To Cindy
Enjoy the Journey
Jesse Avery

She Still Has Flowers in Her Hair

She Still Has Flowers in Her Hair

a soul's journey to self

written and illustrated by Jessie Avery

JPA Associates
Boulder, Colorado

Copyright © 2002 by Jessie P. Avery

All rights reserved. No part of this book may be reproduced in any form or by any electronic or mechanical means, including information storage and retrieval systems, without permission in writing from the publisher, except by a reviewer who may quote brief passages in a review.

Published by:
JPA Associates, 11026 Maple Road
Lafayette, Colorado 80026

ISBN 0-9727125-0-X
Printed in Singapore

page 4 ❖ she still has flowers in her hair

"Now by faith is the assurance of things hoped for, the conviction of things not seen."

— *Hebrews 11:1*

Contents

A New Day
Garden of Este 15
I Smile 17
Who Is There 19

Laughter
My Soul 23
Song in My Heart 25
Moments of Existence 27
To Know You 29

Walls
Structure of Strength 33
Fortress of Life 35
Time Carves Its Face 37
Drawn Together 39
Arch of Time 41
Tapestry of the Heart 43

Dancing
Fly Again 47
Being She 49
Gift of Life 51

Weeds 53

Miracle of Family 55

Daddy 57

Spark of Hope 59

Embrace My Soul 61

Opened Eyes

Metamorphosed Me 65

Haloed in Sun 67

Cocoon of Your Love 69

Life's Joy 71

Willing Sail 73

To be Real 75

*for Bill, Luke, and Tao
my strength and inspiration*

So much of life is an unanswered question. As a fresh sprout of hope, we are born and begin our journey. Pieces of the puzzle are there for discovery as we grow, but it is up to us to put them together the best we can.

We are all travelers in time. The unending circle of life repeats its lessons and we only need to listen. It takes ears and an open, fertile heart to hear. These pages represent the journey of my discovery. I hope some of the pieces fit your puzzle.

—jpa

1 a new day

SHE OPENED HER EYES to a new day. The journey had begun. The dresser, the bed, the vase of flowers (she always had flowers around) all looked comfortably the same. Her eyes floated around the room. Her shelves of books were still happily stacked in her bookcase. Her mind drifted to the places and people living in those volumes. Lives of adventure and intrigue, places of mystery and discovery all there for her to share. Then she thought, "What about my life? Jennie, what have you done with all those dreams? What have I to show?"

Her reverie was cut short by an insistent "Yeow!" from her 12-year-old Siamese cat, Tao. He was standing defiantly at the end of her bed insisting she focus on his magnificent blue eyes.

"OK, OK, Tao," she said. "You have a busy day, so you need me to stop this daydreaming and get going."

The sun was peeking in her window and starting to chase the night's shadows away. A sweet smell of jasmine floated in on a breeze dusting her senses with memory of some of the gentle times in her life. The breeze flirted with her curtains as they floated back and forth across her dresser top. Standing proudly from its position of power, her new antique mirror glinted with the sun's rays. A gift from her mom, the mirror had seen many generations of her family. " Oh, the stories you could tell … " , she told him, but all he did was glitter.

She caught sight of her long blonde hair in the mirror. "Spaghetti hair." That's what her mom had called it. Again an insistent "Yeow!" brought her back to the morning. "Tao, you drive a hard bargain... Wait... Tao, you're right. We don't have any jasmine growing in our garden." The scent was filling the room and calling her outside. She threw on a pair of jeans and a t-shirt. There was only an hour left before she had to be at work, but she skipped out into the hall heading for the back door when her foot collided with a furry streak. "Tao!!" she cried as she fell toward the wall and found herself eye to eye with the normally sedate Siamese. He eyed her carefully, assessing the situation, and then opted to abandon the crazed monkey tactics. Slowly he pulled his pride back together and stalked toward the door. Reassembling her arms and legs, she followed the cat.

As she opened the door, she felt him push past her feet again and saw him disappear into the lilac hedge. Drawn by an unexplainable urge to discover the source of the sweet scent of jasmine, she again followed her confident feline. The branches pulled and the thick leaves covered her face. Pushing through, she suddenly broke through to the other side. She collapsed in amazement. Instead of her little patch of garden, an expanse of formal garden hedges outlined an unending maze of flowers, trees and manicured bushes spread out before her. The scent! The scent wasn't jasmine, but honeysuckle. Its tenacious branches wound themselves into a myriad of forms, carefully trained into trees, hedges and low groundcover, it was everywhere!

Catching her breath, she cautiously followed the nearest corridor of green. Where did Tao go? Why did he want to come here? Where is "here"?

Questions and memories of gardens and flowers in her life flooded her mind...

Joy

Laughter

Rivers of Life

Sparkle through the jungle

Of sweet green.

A maze of hidden ways

Weaving the garden of Este.

A flash of black hidden in the dense hedge drew her irresistibly to a crouch, where she found herself eye to eye with the chiseled black face of a regal cat. Her mind raced...

page 16 ❖ she still has flowers in her hair

Hidden in the green patchwork of jade

The green lustrous eyes

Watch me from a pelt of black.

Who am I that I am not making noise?

Who am I that approaches with the

    dance of caution?

I am your sister,

Oh, Panther of Este.

Your questioning silence

Sings to mine

And

I smile.

She stopped and the cat carefully picked his way from behind the olive tree. He stopped as if to tell her a secret…

I sit

Like the cat

Waiting for my time.

Quiet

Watching

Ready

Cautious, he tiptoes

And

Freezes.

Found in stealth

By another kindred soul.

Not a word said

We blink

And he continues his contemplated tread

And I ?

I too

Rise in my soul

And tiptoe out

To find who is

There.

2 laughter

L AUGHTER. She heard the sparkle of laughter from beyond the hedge. She ran down the maze of green, turning corner upon corner. Suddenly, she found herself face to face with a fountain. Water splashed and played down the curved edges. Drops separated into mist and kissed her face. Other jeweled strands of liquid clung to the carved stone faces and sea shells and raced down the surfaces creating a glaze of shining diamonds. Lost in the fountain, she felt herself melt and her thoughts flow …

she still has flowers in her hair ❖ page 21

Water,

Mother of life,

You have given me new strength.

Your laughter sparkles as you fall,

Sprinkling pieces of vision in my heart.

Your joyful play

With your brother sun

Creates a veritable

Kaleidoscope of sight and sound

That captures my senses

And enchants

My soul.

At the base of the fountain, large glittering pools caught the water as it cascaded down into ripples and set up small waves rolling through the glassy surface. She found herself floating…

The sun kisses the waves.

Each smiles at the next

And all sparkle in laughter

As I joyfully fall into their embrace.

They toss and caress me

As I revel in their wild dance.

Their rhythm pounds in my veins

And their song in my heart.

Gazing up through the swirling prisms, her eyes drew her up out of the pools to the floating drops in the air above her…

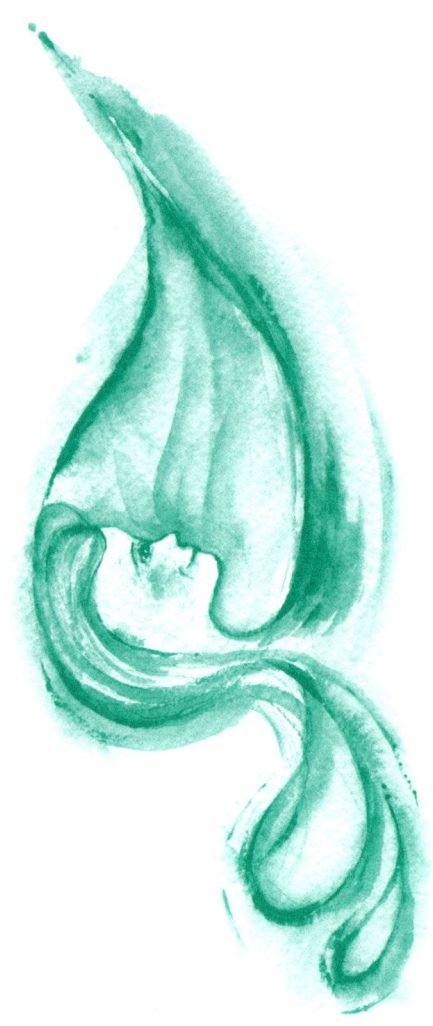

page 26 ❖ *she still has flowers in her hair*

What is my life reflected in a moment?
Held dear and yet far
Seen as a drop
And yet a whole universe unto myself.
What is that thing called life?
What is anyone's possession that makes it
So precious?
Like a box
To be filled.
Like a song
To be sung.
Like a seed
To grow.
Jewels of joy
Carefully chosen and etched with pain
A deep and warm pain
That gives reflection
Splendor
And radiance to the moments of
Existence.

As her thoughts floated with the drops, she gazed once again down at the reflecting pools below her and saw faces gazing back. Dear friends, loved ones blending together to form a gentle face framed with a wisp of blonde hair centered around cautious thoughtful blue eyes. She was looking at a constant changing portrait of herself. Her thoughts drifted to all those precious people in her life…

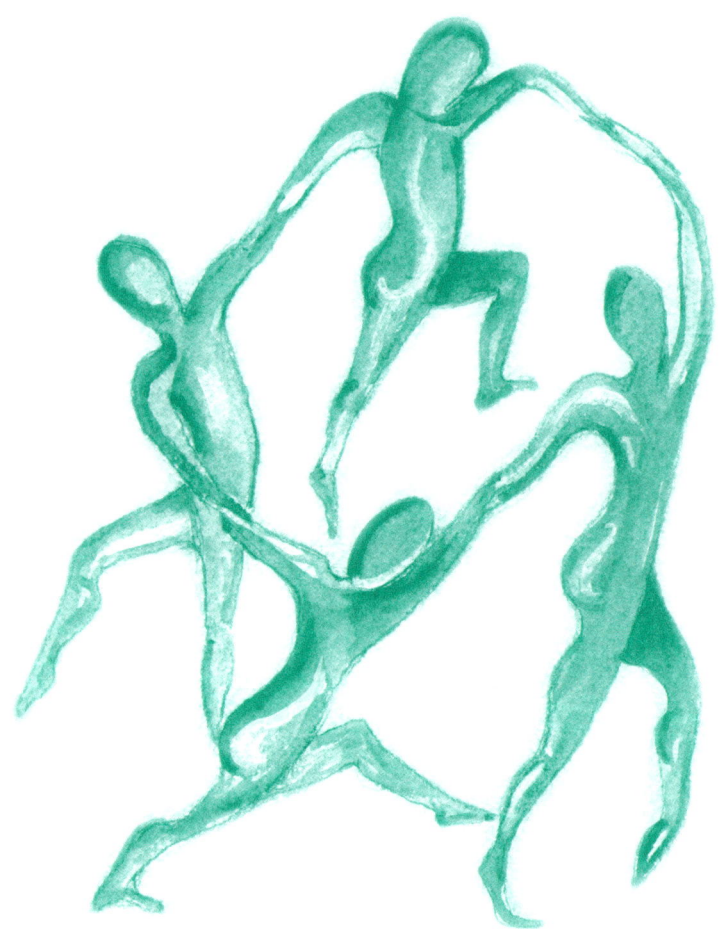

To know you

I would look deep into

Not only your soul,

But the other souls

Whose love paints for me

A portrait of your

Growth.

Their eyes remember your past

And my eyes search their eyes to see

Your future.

3 walls

FLOATING, SUSPENDED IN TIME, she again looked down at the shining pools below her. Rising in reflection, a huge wall of stone began to emerge. The Chateau! The jewel of the garden beckoned her to come and converse. She pulled herself from her watery reverie and found her legs once again under her and moving toward the fortress. As the path rose to the magnificent structure, she found defining stone walls bordering her way. These edges embraced the earth and created terraces for cascades of flowers. The walls themselves drew her to them as she passed and she again felt her mind wander…

page 32 ❖ she still has flowers in her hair

Rocks carefully chosen

Carved to fit each other

Still stand,

Like friendships,

Chosen for their common grain

And cemented with mortar of dust and water.

We, children of dust and water,

Are mortar too.

Tying lives,

Dreams,

And hope,

The rocks of humanity,

Into a structure

Of strength.

Drawn into the walls, she looked deeper into the individual rocks…

page 34 ❖ *she still has flowers in her hair*

Finding the tendency,

Looking for faults,

Time carves the masterpiece.

Where it is weak,

It falls away.

Like the rocks,

We are carved by the pressure

Of our lives.

Shaped by fissures

And chipped to fit our niche

In the fortress of life.

As she once again began moving along the path, she reached out to the top of the stone wall. Her finger trailed behind her and gently drew a path in the light dust. She thought of all the marvelous characters she had encountered in her life and how each had added their own polish to her soul...

page 36 ❖ *she still has flowers in her hair*

Time carves its face upon a rock

Building

Changing

Adding

Subtracting

Bit by bit, blown from afar

Fitting together as edges touch

Yet separated again

Just as quickly

Remembering only the touch

And the small polished spot

Left by the contact

Of the moment.

Souls too,

Brought together in fleeting

Moments of time,

Polishing each other

With the friction of their interaction

And the wisdom of

Combined experience

They become

Smooth and lustrous.

Her heart pounded as she relived fleeting moments of innocent encounter…

Drawn together for a moment

By the muse of chance,

We meet.

Your sparkling smile speaks of flowers

Colors and forms,

Wild and intertwined,

Yet simple in their elegance.

The hand of time designed our

Meeting this once only to swirl our

Lives on to perhaps meet again in another time,

Place

Or life.

Only distance, time and perspective

Will tell.

The way became grander. The path opened to a wide avenue punctuated with terraces and grand views overlooking the expanse of the garden. The Chateau was drawing closer. The towers and arches flowed through the structure creating a rhythm and harmony of an opera.

The drama of life was displayed in the Chateau's theater.

page 40 ❖ she still has flowers in her hair

In your grace and form
I see the centuries
Flow through the lives of your inhabitants.
The wisdom of your lines
And your etched visage
Tell me of the glory and misery
You've seen.
My life,
Just a drop of time in your flow,
Touches the minutes of the many
Who have tasted your
Strength.

She could almost hear the nobles and ladies as they created the tapestry of their lives. She thought of some of her dear friends that, unlike many who had touched her life, were constant, unbending and loyal…

Interwoven,
The strands of friendship's fabric
Paint life's mysterious pattern.
Memories woven with care,
Strand by strand
Forming their unifying whole:
The color of life.
Shining gold from the sunlight of your smile.
Sparkling silver forged from the
    battles we've won.
Warm red that has woven a blanket of care.
Vibrant green that reawakens the life within.
Strong cloth, able to stand the winds of time.
Sometimes a sail:
    To carry us beyond our separate paths.
Sometimes a shelter:
    To guard against the problems that rage.
Timeless, yet built each day,
With the knowledge of
Friendship's trust,
The tapestry of the heart.

4 dancing

SUDDENLY SOMETHING hit her shoulder. A tap, like a reminder from a friend. Who is there? She whirled around. Finding nothing but garden, she looked up. Precariously perched high on a rampart, sat the cat. His luminescent eyes met hers. Tail twitching, he rose and picked his way along the edge of the narrow wall. A few more pebbles rained down, but missed her. She watched intently as the agile tightrope walking cat worked his way down from ledge to ledge. He hesitated. The air became filled with swooping aerialists. Scolding birds, dancing on the breeze, dive bombed the poised predator. Their freedom and passion of purpose drew her spirit into their dance...

page 46 ❖ she still has flowers in her hair

I must fly again.
I feel the winds moving.
I hear the call of the wild.
I know they ask me to come
And I will.
Will you come with me
To seek the sky
And ride the wind?
It can be hard.
The wind will toss you
And the sky is cold in her
Icy blue gown,
But the freedom of flight
Sings in the rhythm of my
Wings
And together we can dance
Across the clouds of storm.

As she twirled and waltzed with the puffs of air currents her soul laughed in recognition…

Pulling away,

Flying again,

The little bird is free.

Reaching for the sky,

Finding a few clouds,

She still fills her lungs with the

Thin, clean air of

Being she.

Filled with the joy of flying free, she suddenly felt the cool embrace of water. Puffs of white encircled her and clouds filled the sky. She felt herself encased in a shimmering cloak of rain. Falling, falling, she looked down as the warm earth reached up to receive her…

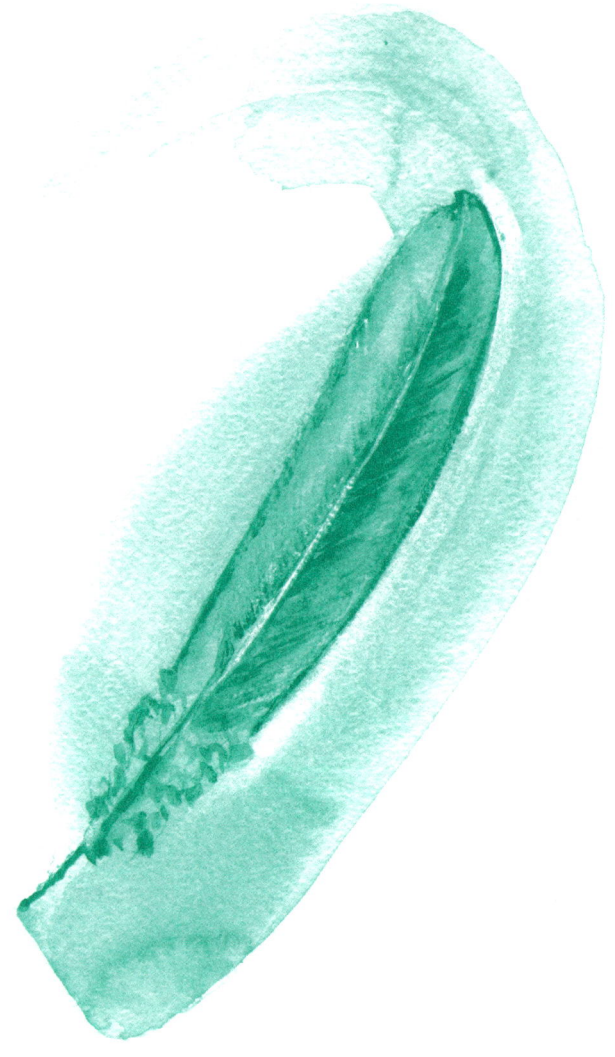

page 50 ❖ *she still has flowers in her hair*

Rain, the gift of life

Falls to give a new clean sheen to

The earth.

But I, a child of the sun,

Search for sister rain's brother,

Looking beyond her clouds

For the smiling warmth of Apollo.

Yet, I know

Each without the other

Makes life useless

And barren.

Finding herself prone, nestled in the earth's fabric, her bug's eye view focused on the sprouting honeysuckle under the manicured hedge…

Let me watch you,
As you reach for the sky,
Tiny buds of new life awaking from
Winter sleep in mother earth.
I celebrate your tenacity.
I long for your freedom.
I give you my heart to teach me to grow
Each unique miracle
To bear a flower of hope.
Weeds,
Some call you weeds,
But like me,
You are sometimes found in places
You don't fit.
Places unplanned,
Yet quietly expressing life's abundance
And mystery.

"Bloom where you are planted," that's what her mom had always told her. Sometimes that's not easy to remember. She felt a velvet paw touch her finger and saw the flicker of a furry tail disappear into the undergrowth. A plaintive growl from behind the leaves called "Follow me…" She scrambled onto her hands and knees and crawled into the tangle of branches. The leaves pulled her clothes and the branches raked her hair. She could catch a note of the feline's song as he easily threaded his way ahead of her. She followed, though the web of interlocked growth held her every move. The smell of honeysuckle was everywhere and the blossoms fell like rain as she pushed on. Her mind wandered to the tangle of family. How each was so different and yet they were tied by the common threads of love and respect…

Threading through the nurture of time

Strength in structure

A web of lives

Are all tied

Yet they are separate…

How do they fit?

Each laces its way through the

Molecules of lifestyle.

Nourishing and living from

The situation of time,

Intertwined,

Careful not to choke,

Forming the ever growing

Miracle of

Family.

She thought of her dad. Strong like the deep roots of these bushes, his presence surrounded her and the maze of branches seemed to melt away...

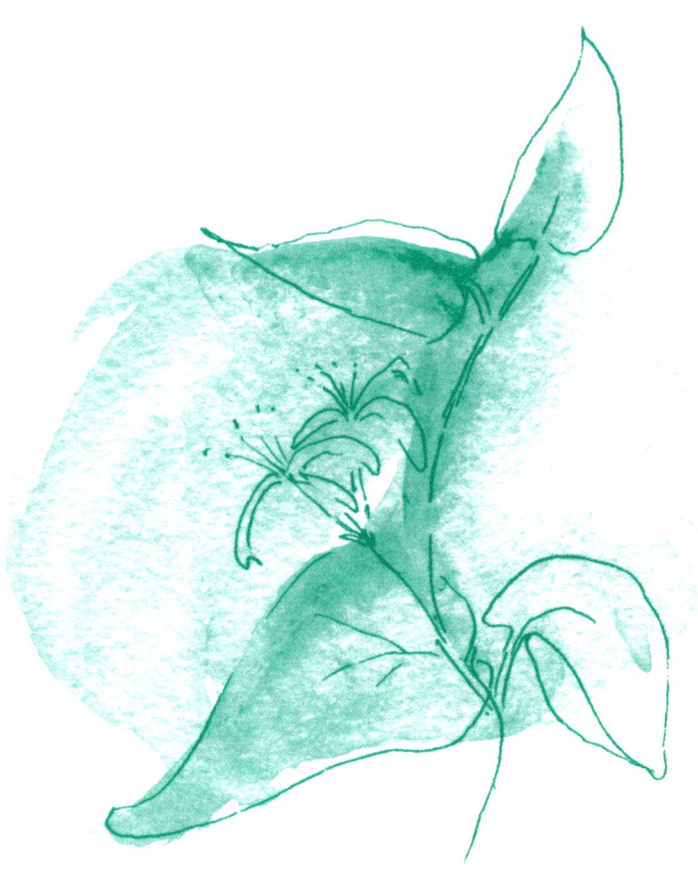

Carefully

Tenderly

Ever present

You have watched and guided

My growth.

Watering

Weeding

Supporting

Your gentle, strong hands

Cradle me.

You let me know I am

Safe...

Safe to explore

Safe to grow

Safe to be me.

You saw the image deep in the raw wood

And carefully set me free.

Thank you

Daddy.

She found herself in a circle of light. The hedges behind her formed a frame for the carefully laid stone walk that encircled a center podium. The marble object was about three feet high and had a copper arrow rising from its center. She picked her way through the circular bed of flowering honeysuckle and gazed down at the arrow. The sun's rays were painting a long shadow on the top of the sundial and pointing to the waning hours left in the day. She looked up and saw the evening star rising even before the night sky had come to hold it…

A flame, reaching for the sky,

A single thought,

An illuminating idea

Given freely to all who would accept it.

A flame reaching for the stars,

Sister flames,

Burning brightly in the dark of night.

A flame warming the air

Giving itself freely

Lighting our way.

Mama, we thank you for your eternal flame.

Never daunted,

Always ready to relight our extinguished hopes.

Your light has always been given freely

To all who would look to see

Light's truth

And the color of life.

Your one small flame

Burning in the candle of wisdom

Has lighted many other lives

With your burning spark of hope.

Thank you.

The shadows got longer and her eyelids grew heavy. She felt the gentle, warm rub of a furry friend. Looking down, she found the glowing eyes of the cat drawing her down to the bed of sweet-smelling flowers. She succumbed and curled up beside the purring pillow…

Gentle blue-black abyss

Cradle me in your eternity.

My eyes reach to you,

Longing to be enfolded in your

Powerful caress.

Luminescent clouds wrap themselves in night

I feel your presence

Walk through the windows of my mind

And softly

Embrace my soul.

5 opened eyes

SHE OPENED HER EYES to a new day. Curled beside her was the snoring body of her life long friend, Tao. She searched the room for clues. Something had happened, but what? Had it been a dream? Was the garden really there or had she imagined it? She looked at Tao. He opened his ice blue eyes and studied her. She stroked his long parallel whiskers. Each strand underlined the thoughts racing through her mind. The strands drew the stanza for the music of his purr.

She looked up and around the room. The dresser, the bed, the vase of flowers all looked somewhat the same, but different. The sunlight bathing the wood in the dresser accented the growth rings and drew a vivid design that she had missed until now. The bed, still warm from her rest, still had the fading mark of her body placed like a fingerprint in the mattress. She ran her hand over the depression and felt the resilient fibers returning to their shape. The vase, filled with zinnias, smiled in the filtered drops of sunlight awaking the room.

Tao got up and stretched, a long humpbacked affair complete with each paw placing its mark on her pillow. A sneaking whiff of honeysuckle floated into the room with the breeze as it played with the curtain.

She got up and gazed into the antique mirror on her dresser. The face looking back was somewhat the same, but different. The long blonde hair was the same, but there were tiny blossoms of honeysuckle clinging to the strands and the mouth was curled up in a smile…

page 64 ❖ she still has flowers in her hair

Covering miles

Translating time

New cultures gone

Old to return

But what is new and what is old?

Time adrift.

I search with eyes made new

To see familiarity.

My ears listen for the sound,

Tapestry of home.

But the new ears hear the old

Sounds differently.

A stranger in my own life.

I look for familiarity

And find a metamorphosed

Me.

She looked closer at the blossoms in her hair, each perfect in its crimson trumpet. The soft feel of the flowers spoke of a youth and freshness of ever changing life.

Tapping

Asking

Explaining

Readjusting

My old roots still draw from the

Aquifer of care,

But, each new leaf

Each new blossom must be presented

To explain the new outline haloed

In sun.

She found Tao rubbing on her leg and reached down to pick him up. He purred with contentment and looked at her with wise knowing eyes…

Again I see myself

As I look through your eyes.

Again I feel the warmth of the

Woven threads of care:

Your wisdom and

Strength.

Enfold my tattered spirit

And regenerate me once again

To fly forth from the

Cocoon of your love.

What was real? She stroked the chocolate fur where it blended into the mocha mantle of his coat. "Tao, you're telling me who Jennie is, but why can't I believe you?" His tail curled into its accustomed smile and he melted in a pool of purr.

You ask no extra measure

But you gladly give support and constant

Nourishment.

Tap roots for my structure,

I reach through you to the

Unending aquifer of

Life's joy.

Her reverie was cut short by the call of the rooster outside. Calling his hens, declaring his being and noting that time was draining from the present to the future as she communed with her soulmate. Yes, time was fleeting, but was it really? Hadn't she been in time last night, or was it this morning? Past, present and future all woven together with perception and perspective. She suddenly felt the freedom of her soul's flight.

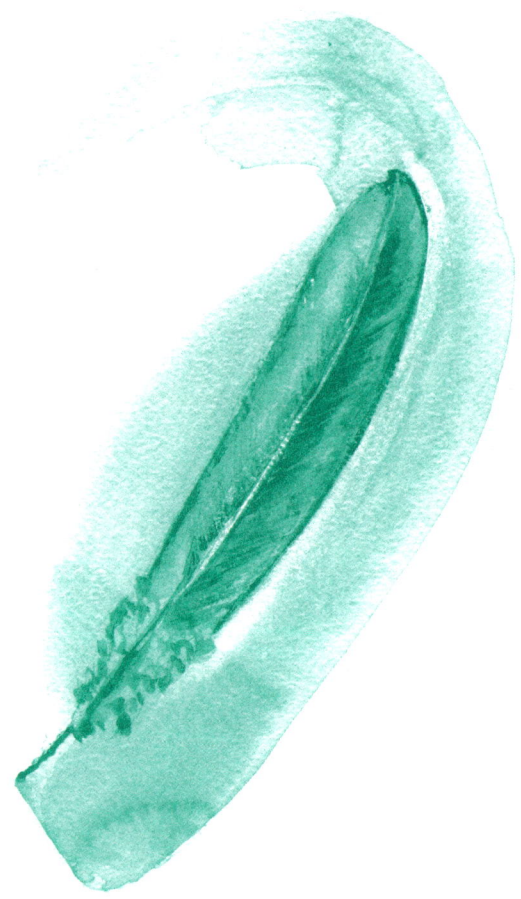

Flying in the tempest of my soul,

I sweep through the drifts of time,

Once again free of the life's daily snag.

I follow your puffs of inspiration.

Feeling their guidance

Both gentle and abrupt

Knowing wind never

Deserts a willing

Sail.

She knew life was there for her to make it what she wanted. No longer bound by time and the perception of space, she knew she really did still have flowers in her hair and they were real.

I have loved you.

Shown you the flowers of morning,

But only in remembrance

And faith do they live.

Their strength lies not in this

World, but in

The one to come.

Let us believe,

My love,

And know the garden to be

Real.

she still has flowers in her hair ❖ *page 77*

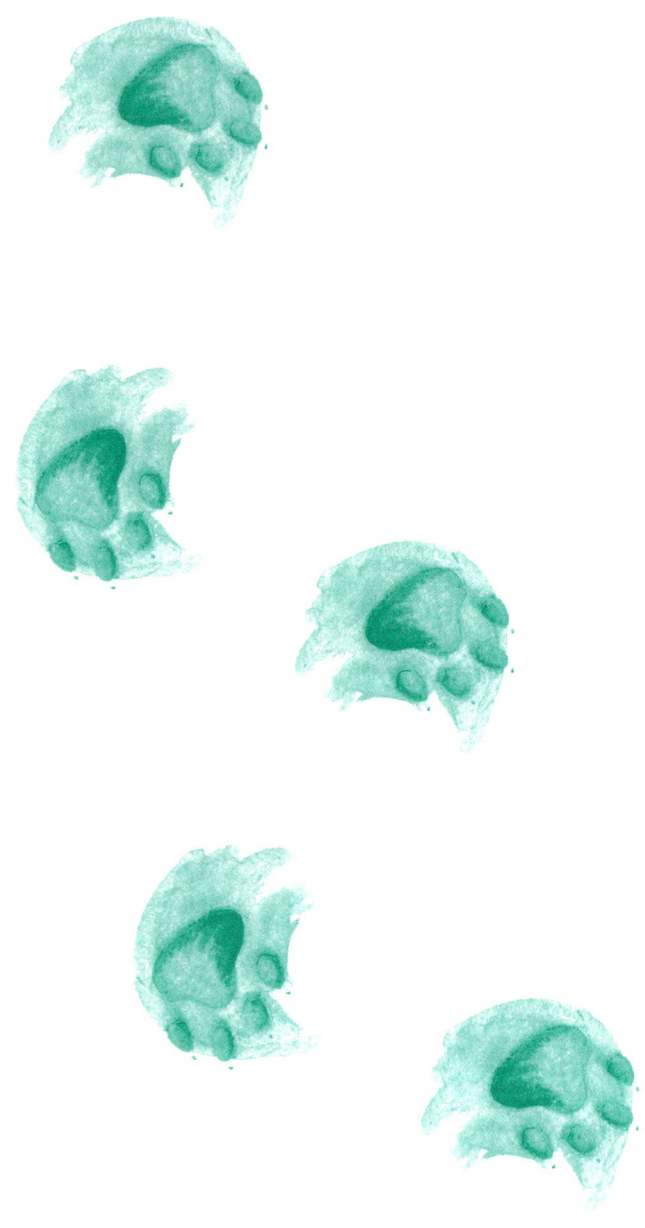

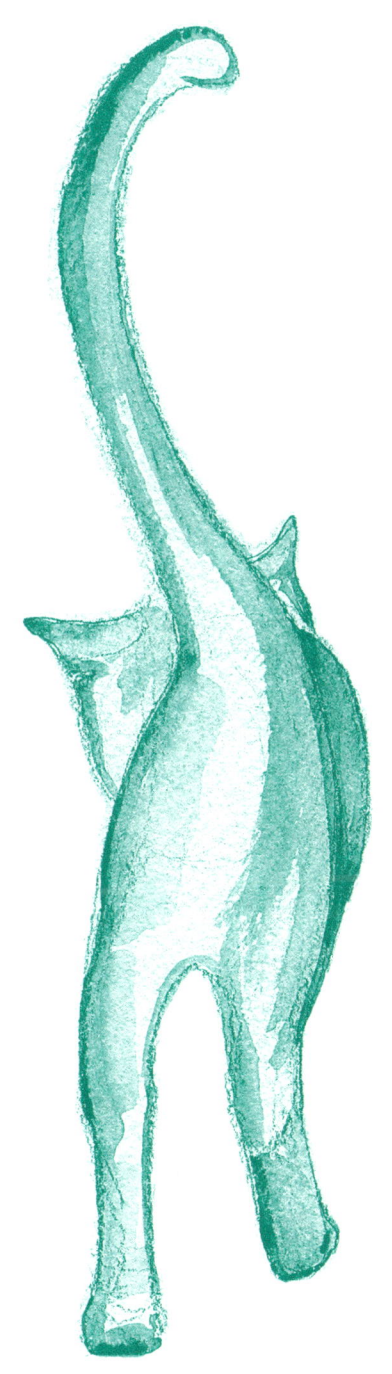

she still has flowers in her hair ❖ *page 79*